Vegetarian Pressure Cooker Recipe Book: 50 High Pressure Recipes for Busy People

By Maria Holmes

Table of Contents

Preface

Dear Reader!

I would like to take this opportunity to thank you for taking the time to read my book and hope that you find these pressure cooker recipes interesting and tasty!

Before we start exploring the wonders of the pressure cooker I would like to introduce myself. My name is Maria Holmes and I am indeed the author of this pressure cooker recipe book that you are now reading. If you are interested in learning more about me, my mission and my passion, please join my Facebook community at _Homes Cooked Meals_ for interesting activities and enthusiastic discussions. Or you might want to visit my blog at www.holmescookedmeals.com.

But let's get back to the topic at hand: The versatile pressure cooker!

Many modern food authorities consider the pressure cooker an absolutely essential part of a well-equipped kitchen. Are you surprised? You shouldn't be. Though a few folks may think of the pressure cooker as a relic, the truth is, its numerous advantages have never gone out of style.

Pressure cooking saves time and energy by cooking foods three to ten times faster than ordinary methods. It's even faster than a microwave for many foods! With much less water used in cooking and a fully insulated external pot, much less energy is required, saving up to 70% of energy when compared with boiling, steaming, oven cooking or slow cooking. Electric pressure cookers are the second most energy efficient cooking appliance after microwaves.

Valuable nutrients, food flavors and garden-fresh colors are also preserved by using a pressure cooker. Several foods, or even an entire meal, can be prepared at the same time in one pan. And, most importantly, foods cooked in the pressure cooker taste great.

While pressure cooking may not be the end all solution to healthy eating, it is an important tool that should not go underestimated. Food and cooking is a process of discovery. I've discovered the joy and advantages of cooking with a pressure cooker and I hope you do too.

Now go into the kitchen, knowing that you can get that meal onto the table in 10 to 30 minutes. Bon Appétit!

Enjoy and be well!

Maria Holmes

Acknowledgement

I would like to express my gratitude to my parents, who have always supported and encouraged me in everything I have done in my life. Without their love and support, this book might never have been written.

I am also grateful to my dear friends who I often use as test subjects when developing my recipes. Without their help and sacrifice, many of these recipes may have turned out bland and tasteless. Many of these friends have become members and supporters of my Facebook Page and blog at www.holmescookedmeals.com.

And a special thank you goes out to my loving husband and my two amazing children (Ellie an Isaac) who endlessly encourage me to share my love for food and my many recipes with the world.

And most importantly, thank you, dear reader, for purchasing my *Vegetarian Pressure Cooker Recipe Book: 50 High Pressure Recipes for Busy People*.

What Food is Best Prepared in a Pressure Cooker?

While the pressure cooker is a wonderfully versatile appliance, it is better for some types of food than others. For example, it is ideal for just about any comfort food – soups, stews, and creamy risottos. Not only does it give you perfect results, you can cut the usual cooking time down by two-thirds.

Beans, soups, stews, chilies and grains are also perfect candidates for you pressure cooker.

And don't forget desserts. It makes wonderful rice pudding, crème caramel and steamed Christmas pudding in a fraction of the time you're used to.

Or you can use the cooker as a tool to prep ingredients – dried chickpeas for hummus, beans and whole grains for healthy salads, and cooked fruits for preserves. Beans can be instantly quick-soaked in the pressure cooker, most varieties in less than a minute.

The pressure cooker is perfect for making rich homemade stocks with recycled vegetable scraps. Corn-on-the-cob never touches water when steamed in its own juice on the trivets in less than 2 minutes.

Cooking under high pressure helps retain water-soluble nutrients that are normally boiled away, and instantly infuses and mingles flavors in a way that is usually found only in slow-cooked foods. And unlike other appliances (like slow cookers), you can brown vegetables in the pan before pressure cooking, adding extra layers of flavor that comes from caramelizing sugars.

Adapting Conventional Recipes for the Pressure Cooker

Almost any recipe that requires long and slow cooking, simmering, braising or steaming can easily be adapted for pressure cooking.

Think of all of your favorite peasant cuisines from braised Spanish beans to slow-simmered Indian curries. You probably have many favorite family recipes that your mother or grandmother served which could be completed in less than half the traditional time in a pressure cooker.

One of the main differences between conventional and pressure cooking recipes is the amount of liquid required. In the pressure cooker, most stews need less than 2 cups (500 ml) broth, stewed tomatoes, coconut milk, or other saucy ingredients. Remember that vegetables will release liquid while cooking, about 1/4 cup (50 ml) for every 2 cups (500 ml) of raw veggies.

Plan to thicken your dishes at the end of the cooking process. I have found that a flour roux used at the start of my favorite Cajun-style vegetarian stews and gumbos burned in the intense heat of the pressure cooker. The solution: make the roux on the side and whisk it into the stew after the pressure has been released.

Pressure cooking also requires a different approach to using herbs and spices. The high heat of pressure cooking destroys the flavor in delicate herbs, and even the most robust herbs if used fresh. Plan to use dried herbs in your recipes (and in greater quantities), or add your fresh chopped herbs at the end of cooking.

Steps to Successful Pressure Cooking

Cooking under pressure is easy if you follow a few simple steps.

Browning (where appropriate). While it's not absolutely necessary to brown vegetables before pressure cooking, I heartily recommend it. Most stews and soups benefit from the added flavor that comes with browning and caramelizing sugars before cooking.

Filling. Don't overfill the pressure cooker. Make sure the pot is never more than two-thirds full. If you are cooking beans, rice or grains (which foam up during cooking), make sure the pot is no more than half full. Some cookers have a maximum fill indicator line stamped on the pot. Conversely, be sure you don't underfill the cooker. Consult the manufacturer's instruction booklet to determine the minimum amount of liquid required for pressure cooking in your unit, usually at least 1/2 to 1 cup (125 to 250 ml).

If you are steaming food on a rack, place a metal trivet or steaming basket inside the unit, add the water and place the food directly on the rack or in a heatproof plate or casserole dish. The trivet or basket is designed to keep the water level below the food you are cooking – so don't add too much water.

Lock the lid. Make sure the lid is properly closed before putting the pressure cooker on the heat. Some pressure cookers have dots or marks you will need to line up before twisting the lid to lock it. With others, you pull a lever across or push a button to activate the lock.

Bring the cooker to full pressure. Get the pressure cooker up to full pressure as quickly as possible by putting it over high heat. If you have a multi-level valve, choose the appropriate "psi" setting. It can take several minutes to achieve full pressure. Use a burner that is no larger than the base of the pot and, if you are cooking with gas, be sure the flames are not licking up the sides. You can tell when the cooker is up to full pressure in several ways. New models have a button that rises to indicate that pressure had been reached, and will hiss slightly until you reduce the heat. On old jiggle-top models, the weight will begin to jiggle rapidly; reduce the heat immediately or you will have a blow-out. *Reduce heat, just to maintain even pressure*. Once the cooker is up to pressure, reduce the heat to low or medium-low. You want to maintain an even pressure during cooking, but you should not hear too much steam escaping (an indication that the heat is too high). With a jiggle-top model, the jiggler should just barely continue to rock, about 4 or 5 times a minute. Fixed weight valve should not sputter but may emit a very soft hissing sound, while a spring-valve cooker will be quite silent, with its valve stem rising to the desired level without dropping.

Watch the cooking time. All the cooking times specified in the following recipes are from the moment the pressure cooker is up to pressure to the time the pressure should be released. Begin timing when the unit is up to pressure and use an accurate timer (I use the timer on my microwave) to make sure that you release the pressure as soon as the time is up. If you are pressure cooking at high altitude, you will have to adjust the cooking times. Add about 5 percent more time for every 1,000 feet (30 meters) above sea level. If you find the food is not properly cooked when you remove the lid, lock the lid back in place, bring the pressure cooker back up to full pressure over high heat, reduce the heat to low and cook for another 1 or 2 minutes longer. You can also finish the cooking conventionally; this is especially desirable if you want to reduce the cooking liquid to thicken a sauce or stew.

Release the pressure. When the instructions in a recipe call for releasing the pressure naturally, simply remove the pressure cooker from the heat and wait for the pressure indicator to drop. When the pressure has dissipated, the locking mechanism (on those cookers so equipped) disengages and you can remove the lid. Tilt the lid away from you when opening it. The "natural release" method is best for beans and grains, which can break up and clog the valve if you release the pressure quickly. This method also keeps fragile items like beans intact. It is also good for soups and stocks, which can spew out when the pressure is released too quickly.

If the recipe calls for releasing the pressure quickly (appropriate for many dishes and those that might overcook if left under pressure), simply release the pressure valve by pressing the button or flipping the lever. A steady jet of steam will flow out of the machine until all of the pressure has been released. (Be careful, the steam can be hot!) Then the pressure indicator/locking mechanism button will drop and allow you to remove the lid.

If the cooker doesn't have a quick-release valve, you will have to take it to the sink and run cold water over the lid, being careful not to run water into the steam valve, until you hear the locking mechanism release. Some models do not have a locking mechanism to prevent opening the unit while there is still pressure inside. If the lid is removed before all of the pressure has dissipated, the food inside can erupt and burn you. Be careful.

Tips for Preparing Beans

Soaking methods. All beans need to soak before cooking. Soaking rehydrates the beans and helps to remove some of the complex sugars that give beans a bad name in polite company. There are several procedures for soaking beans which are described below.

TRADITIONAL SOAKING – If you have time, just put your beans in a pot with three or four times their volume in water and let them sit for 4 to 8 hours at room temperatures.

QUICK SOAKING – To speed up the soaking process, you can place the beans and water in a pot and bring them to a full, rolling boil. Simmer the beans for 2 minutes, then remove the pot from the heat, cover it, and let the beans soak for 1 hour. Drain away those gaseous complex carbs and proceed with your recipe.

PRESSURE SOAKING – You can speed up the soaking process even further by using the pressure cooker. Place the beans and water in a pressure cooker (3 cups [750 ml] water for every cup [250 ml] beans, plus 1 tablespoon (15 ml) vegetable oil if you have a jiggle-top cooker). Lock the lid in place and bring up to full pressure over high heat. What you do next depends on the size and type of beans you are preparing.

* For small beans, remove the cooker from the heat immediately and let the pressure come down naturally for 10 minutes before releasing the remaining steam using the quick-release valve.

* For larger beans, cook under pressure for 1 minute, then allow the pressure to come down naturally for 10 minutes.

* For chickpeas and very large beans, cook for 2 to 3 minutes on high pressure before allowing the pressure to come down naturally for 10 minutes, then release any remaining pressure with the quick-release valve.

Checking if beans are fully soaked. The goal of soaking is to have water penetrate to the center of the bean. You can check this by cutting one open to make sure the color is even. An opaque spot in the center indicates the bean needs further soaking, or that you will have to add a few minutes of cooking time while pressure cooking the beans.

Special precautions for pressure cooking beans and lentils. If you like legumes or cook a lot of vegetarian dishes, the pressure cooker is a miracle. It allows you to cook inexpensive and healthy dried beans in minutes. Still, there are some precautions to take when you're cooking beans and lentils under pressure.

LEAVE ROOM FOR THE BEANS TO COOK – Make sure you never overload the pressure cooker when cooking beans. Because beans and lentils froth up and expand substantially (up to 4 times their dry size and weight) while cooking, never fill the pressure cooker more than one-third full.

USE ENOUGH WATER – Always use at least 2 cups (500 ml) of water or other liquid for every 1 cup (250 ml) of dry beans in a recipe. If you have an old-fashioned jiggle-top pressure cooker, always watch it carefully while cooking beans, since the vent can easily become clogged. If it does, you will hear a loud hissing noise. Immediately remove the cooker from the heat and release the pressure. As noted above in the section on soaking beans, jiggle-top pressure cooker users should add 1 tablespoon (15 ml) of oil to the beans and water before cooking to help reduce foaming and potential clogging.

WATCH YOUR COOKING TIME - Cooking time for beans can vary substantially, depending on a variety of factors, such as the age and dryness of the beans. Even local humidity can affect cooking times. Where a recipe offers a range of cooking time, it's always best to start with the shorter one. You can always finish the beans conventionally or add another minute or two of pressure cooking if they are not quite done. To check for doneness, cut a bean in half with a sharp knife and look at the center. If the beans are done, they will be one color throughout, and tender.

LET PRESSURE DROP NATURALLY – When the cooking time is complete, remove the cooker from the heat and allow it to stand until the pressure indicator drops. This helps to avoid clogging the center pipe and safety valve with pulpy cooking liquid. It also prevents the beans from splitting.

KEEP YOUR COOKER CLEAN – Always clean the pressure regulator and lid carefully after cooking beans to make sure there are no obstructions.

NO SALT – Never add salt to a bean recipe before cooking. If you do, the beans can become tough and never really soften properly.

Appetizers

THE RECIPES

Hummus

Cooking time: 15 minutes
Makes about 3 cups (750 ml)

This Mediterranean spread is perfect with warm triangles of pita bread or veggies for dipping. This is a good, basic recipe for hummus. When you want a change in flavor and color, try adding 1/2 cup (125 ml) roasted red pepper or 1/2 cup (125 ml) chopped parsley (or even roasted garlic) before puréeing the mixture.

Ingredients

1 cup (250 ml) dried chickpeas
1 teaspoon (5 ml) ground cumin
1 teaspoon (5 ml) salt
1/4 cup (50 ml) extra virgin olive oil
1/4 cup (50 ml) tahini paste (sesame seed paste)
2 teaspoons (10 ml) sesame oil
Juice of 2 large lemons
3 cloves garlic, minced
1/4 cup (50 ml) warm water (approximate)

Directions

Soak the chickpeas overnight in water to cover or use the quick pressure-soak method* then drain.

In a pressure cooker, cover the chickpeas with at least 1-inch (2.5 cm) of water then lock the lid in place and bring the cooker up to full pressure over high heat. Reduce the heat to medium-low, just to maintain even pressure, and cook for 15 minutes.

Remove from heat and release the pressure quickly then drain.

Combine the chickpeas, cumin, salt, olive oil, tahini paste, sesame oil, lemon juice and the garlic in a food processor and purée until smooth. (If the mixture seems too dry, add enough of the warm water as necessary to thin.)

Serve immediately with warm pita bread or refrigerate.

*For further directions please refer to the Pressure Soaking instructions found in the "Introduction" section of the book.

Dhal Dip with Pappadums

Cooking time: 8 minutes
Makes about 2 cups (500 ml)

This is the perfect starter for an Indian meal. Serve the spicy split-pea spread with crispy pappadums and sliced peppers, green beans and zucchini sticks for dipping. Or spread it on a pita and top with grilled vegetables for an exotic vegetarian wrap.

Ingredients

1 tablespoon (15 ml) olive oil
1 teaspoon (5 ml) butter
1 small onion chopped
2 teaspoons (10 ml) mince ginger root
1 clove garlic, minced
1 serrano chili pepper seeded and minced
1/2 teaspoon (2 ml) garam masala
1/4 teaspoon (1 ml) ground turmeric
1/2 teaspoon (2 ml) dry mustard
1 cup (250 ml) dried yellow split peas
2 cups (500 ml) water
1/4 cup (50 ml) plain yogurt or sour cream
2 tablespoons (25 ml) chopped cilantro

Directions

In a pressure cooker, heat the olive oil and butter over medium heat then add the onion, ginger, garlic, and serrano chili and sauté until soft.

Stir in the garam masala, turmeric and dry mustard and cook for 1 minute or until the spices are fragrant.

Stir in the split peas and add the water.

Lock the lid in place and bring the cooker up to full pressure over high heat then reduce the heat to medium-low just to maintain even pressure, and cook for 8 minutes.

Remove from heat and allow the pressure to drop naturally.

Transfer to a bowl.

Stir the dhal until cooled and thickened then whisk in the yogurt until the mixture is smooth and stir in the cilantro.

Serve with pappadums for dipping.

Spiced Chickpeas

Cooking time: 15 minutes
Makes 2 to 3 cups (500 to 750 ml)

Here, cooked chickpeas are slowly sautéed with Indian spices until they are golden brown and crisp. This addictive vegetarian snack is great served with beer or cocktails.

Ingredients

1 cup (250 ml) dried chickpeas
4 cups (1 L) water
1 small onion, peeled
1 bay leaf
1/4 cup (50 ml) butter
2 tablespoons (25 ml) olive oil
1 teaspoon (5 ml) minced garlic
1 teaspoon (5 ml) onion salt
1 teaspoon (5 ml) ground ginger
1 teaspoon (5 ml) ground turmeric
1/2 teaspoon (2 ml) coriander
1/4 teaspoon (1 ml) cayenne pepper (or to taste)
1 tablespoon (15 ml) kosher salt

Directions

Soak the chickpeas in water to cover or use the quick pressure soaking method* then drain.

In a pressure cooker, combine the chickpeas, water, onion and bay leaf then lock the lid in place and bring the cooker up to full pressure over high heat. Reduce the heat to medium-low, just to maintain even pressure, and cook for 15 minutes.

Remove from heat and allow the pressure to drop naturally.

Drain the chickpeas well and discard the onion and bay leaf.

In a small pot over medium heat or in a bowl in the microwave, melt the butter and stir in the olive oil and garlic.

In a large bowl, toss the chickpeas with the garlic mixture then combine the onion salt, ginger, turmeric, coriander and cayenne and sprinkle the spice mixture over the chickpeas, tossing to coat.

Spread the chickpeas in a single layer on one or two large rimmed baking sheets then bake in a preheated 400°F (200°C) oven for 5 to 10 minutes until brown and crisp, shaking the pan or stirring the peas often so that they brown evenly and don't burn.

Transfer to a large bowl and toss with kosher salt.

Serve the chickpeas hot or at room temperature.

To reheat, spread on a rimmed baking sheet and bake in a preheated 350°F (180°C) oven for 5 to 10 minutes.

* For further directions please refer to the Pressure Soaking instructions found in the "Introduction" section of this book.

White Bean Dip

Cooking time: 12 to 13 minutes (for Great Northern beans) or 8 to 9 minutes (for navy beans)
Makes about 2 cups (500 ml)

For a slightly more Mediterranean version, substitute dried thyme for cumin and chopped basil for cilantro. Gently heat the dip to warm it, then mix in a few ounces of crumbled goat cheese or feta cheese and serve with pita wedges.

Ingredients

3/4 cup (175 ml) dried white beans, such as Great Northern or navy beans
2 cloves garlic
3 tablespoons (45 ml) lemon juice
1/3 cup (75 ml) extra virgin olive oil
2 teaspoons (10 ml) ground cumin
1-1/2 teaspoons (7 ml) chili powder
Pinch red pepper flakes
3 tablespoons (45 ml) minced cilantro
Salt and freshly ground black pepper to taste

Directions

Soak the beans overnight in water to cover or use the quick pressure-soaking method* then drain.

In a pressure cooker, cover the beans with at least 1-inch (2.5 cm) of water then lock the lid in place and bring the cooker up to full pressure over high heat. Reduce the heat to medium-low, just to maintain even pressure and cook for 12 to 13 minutes for Great Northern beans or 8 to 9 minutes for navy beans.

Remove from heat and allow the pressure to drop naturally then drain the beans and rinse under cold running water to cool them quickly.

In a food processor, drop the cloves of garlic through the feed tube with the machine running to chop then add the beans, lemon juice, olive oil, cumin, chili powder, and red pepper flakes and purée until smooth.

Fold in the cilantro and season to taste with salt and pepper.

Serve with taco chips or fresh vegetables.

* For further directions please refer to the Pressure Soaking instructions found in the "Introduction" section of this book.

Eggplant Caponata

Cooking time: 4 to 5 minutes
Makes 4 cups (1 L)

Caponata is the Sicilian version of French ratatouille. Serve it on toast for an hors d'oeuvre or tossed with hot pasta for a speedy main course.

Ingredients

1 large eggplant, skin on, cut into 1-inch (2.5 cm) cubes
2 teaspoons (10 ml) salt
1 tablespoon (15 ml) packed brown sugar
2 tablespoons (25 ml) tomato paste
2 tablespoons (25 ml) balsamic vinegar
1/2 cup (125 ml) olive oil
1 onion, chopped
1 small red bell pepper, chopped
1 small yellow bell pepper, chopped
1 cup (250 ml) canned crushed tomatoes
1/2 cup (125 ml) air-cured black olives, pitted and chopped
2 tablespoons (25 ml) chopped basil

Directions

Toss the eggplant with salt then transfer to a colander and let stand for 30 minutes. Rinse and drain well then pat dry with paper towels.

In a bowl, whisk together the brown sugar, tomato paste and vinegar and set aside.

In a pressure cooker, heat the olive oil over high heat then add the eggplant and sauté for 2 minutes.

Stir in the onion, red and yellow peppers and tomatoes then lock the lid in place and bring the cooker up to full pressure over high heat. Reduce the heat to medium-low, just to maintain even pressure and cook for 4 to 5 minutes.

Remove from heat and release the pressure quickly.

Stir to break up the eggplant slightly then stir in the reserved tomato-paste mixture, olives and basil.

Allow to cool.

Serve at room temperature or chilled. (It will keep, covered, in the refrigerator for up to 4 days.)

Soups

THE RECIPES

Curried Cauliflower Soup

Cooking time: 8 minutes
Serves 4

The spices and small red lentils combine to give this soup a lively golden color and a hearty texture. If you have a couple of cups of leftover cooked rice, stir it in for an even more substantial soup.

Ingredients

4 cloves garlic, peeled
1 1-inch (2.5 cm) piece ginger, peeled
1 medium onion, chopped
1/4 cup (50 ml) water
2 tablespoons (25 ml) canola oil
1 teaspoon (5 ml) ground cumin
1 teaspoon (5 ml) coriander
1 teaspoon (5 ml) turmeric
1/4 teaspoon (1 ml) cayenne pepper
2 cups (500 ml) chopped cauliflower
4 cups (1 L) vegetable stock or water
1/2 cup (125 ml) split red lentils
Salt, freshly ground black pepper, and freshly squeezed lime juice to taste

Directions

In a blender, combine the garlic, ginger, onion and water, then purée to a paste and set aside.

Heat the oil in a pressure cooker over medium-high heat, then add the cumin, coriander, turmeric and cayenne and cook together for 30 seconds.

Add the cauliflower and the reserved onion paste and cook, stirring for 5 minutes longer, until the onions begin to brown.

Add the stock and lentils to the pot then lock the lid in place and bring up to high pressure over high heat. Reduce the heat to medium-low, just to maintain pressure, and cook for 8 minutes.

Let the pressure drop naturally.

Season with the salt, pepper and a squeeze of lime juice.

Mexican Pinto Bean Soup

Cooking time: 10 minutes
Serves 4 to 6

Hearty and filling, this soup is the perfect antidote to a case of the mid-winter blues.

Ingredients

1 cup (250 ml) dried pinto beans
2 cloves garlic, divided
1 large onion, halved, divided
1 tablespoon (15 ml) vegetable oil
1 teaspoon (5 ml) salt
2 tablespoons (25 ml) olive oil or vegetable oil
1/3 cup (75 ml) whipping (35%) cream
Grated Monterey Jack cheese, cilantro sprigs and diced avocado for garnish

Directions

Soak the beans overnight in water to cover or use the quick pressure-soak method* then drain.

In a pressure cooker, cover the beans with at least 1-inch (2.5 cm) of water then add 1 clove garlic, half the onion and the vegetable oil.

Lock the lid in place and bring the cooker up to full pressure over high heat then reduce the heat to medium-low, just to maintain even pressure, and cook for 10 minutes.

Remove from heat and release the pressure quickly.

The beans should be very soft. If not, lock the lid in place and return to full pressure and cook for 2 to 3 minutes longer. Remove from heat and release the pressure quickly.

Drain the beans, reserving the cooking liquid.

In a food processor, purée the bean mixture, adding some of the reserved liquid as necessary to make smooth.

Meanwhile, mince the remaining onion and garlic.

In a large pot, heat the oil over medium heat then add the onion and garlic and sauté for about 5 minutes or until golden.

Add the puréed bean mixture to the pot along with enough of the reserved liquid to make a smooth soup.

Bring to a boil and simmer for 10 minutes.

Season with salt and pepper then add the cream and simmer until thickened and smooth.

Serve individual bowls of soup topped with a handful of grated cheese, a few cubes of avocado and a sprig of cilantro.

*For further directions please refer to the Pressure Soaking instructions found in the "Introduction" section of this book.

Root Vegetable Soup

Cooking time: 7 minutes
Serves 4

Flavorful root vegetables are available at all times of the year for this creamy, elegant soup, which is deceptively low in fat. If you're using dried dill, add it before pressure cooking.

Ingredients

2 teaspoons (10 ml) vegetable oil or butter
1 clove garlic, minced
1 cup (250 ml) chopped onions
3 cups (750 ml) chicken stock
1 potato, peeled and chopped
3/4 cup (175 ml) chopped carrots
3/4 cup (175 ml) peeled chopped sweet potato
1/2 cup (125 ml) chopped parsnip
2 tablespoons (25 ml) chopped dill (or 2 teaspoon (10 ml) dried)
Salt and white pepper to taste

Directions

In a pressure cooker, heat the oil over medium heat then add the garlic and onion and sauté for about 5 minutes or until tender.

Add the chicken stock, potato, carrot, sweet potato and parsnip.

Lock the lid in place and bring the cooker up to full pressure over high heat then reduce the heat to medium-low, just to maintain even pressure, and cook for 7 minutes.

Remove from heat and release the pressure quickly.

In a food processor or with an immersion blender, purée the vegetables with some of the cooking liquid until smooth then return the purée to the pot and stir to mix with the remaining liquid. Bring to a boil.

Stir in the dill and season with salt and white pepper just before serving.

Thai Green Curry and Sweet Potato Soup

Cooking time: 3 minutes
Serves 4

For an even spicier version of this flavorful Asian soup, use a Thai red curry paste instead of the green variety. Both are available in jars or packets at Asian markets or the Asian-food section of many large supermarkets.

Ingredients

2 tablespoons (25 ml) vegetable oil
3 red, yellow or orange bell peppers, cut into slivers
2 cloves garlic, minced
1 large onion, slivered
1 tablespoon (15 ml) Thai green curry paste
2 sweet potatoes, peeled and cubed
1 can (14 ounces [398 ml]) unsweetened coconut milk
1/4 cup (50 ml) water
1 teaspoon (5 ml) lemon or lime juice
1 cup (250 ml) snow peas or green beans, cut into 1-inch lengths
1 tablespoon (15 ml) chopped cilantro

Directions

In a pressure cooker, heat the oil over medium heat then add the peppers, garlic, and onion and sauté for 5 minutes.

Stir in the curry paste and cook for 1 minute.

Add the sweet potatoes, coconut milk, water and lemon juice.

Lock the lid in place and bring the cooker up to full power over medium-high heat then reduce the heat to medium-low just to maintain even pressure, and cook for 3 minutes.

Remove from heat and release the pressure quickly.

Stir in the snow peas, cover and cook (not under pressure) for 2 to 3 minutes, or just until the vegetables are tender-crisp.

Stir in the cilantro before serving.

Beet and Vegetable Borscht

Cooking time: 10 minutes
Serves 8

This is an old-fashioned soup, brought from Canada by immigrants from the Ukraine, Romania and other parts of Eastern Europe.

Ingredients

1 tablespoon (15 ml) butter
2 cloves garlic, minced
1 large onion, minced
3 cups (750 ml) cubed peeled potatoes (preferably a waxy red variety)
1 cup (250 ml) chopped carrots
3 or 4 medium beets, unpeeled with 1-inch (2.5 cm) of tops intact
4 cups (1 L) shredded purple cabbage
8 cups (2 L) vegetable stock or water
1 can (14 ounces [398 ml]) tomatoes, crushed
1 tablespoon (15 ml) balsamic or red wine vinegar
Salt to taste
Freshly ground black pepper to taste
Paprika to taste
2 tablespoons (25 ml) chopped dill
1/2 cup (125 ml) sour cream
2 tablespoons (25 ml) all-purpose flour

Directions

In a pressure cooker, melt the butter over medium heat then add the garlic and onion and sauté for about 5 minutes or until the onion starts to brown.

Stir in the potatoes and carrots and sauté for 3 minutes.

Add the beets, cabbage, stock and tomatoes.

Lock the lid in place and bring the cooker up to full pressure over high heat then reduce the heat to medium-low, just to maintain even pressure and cook for 10 minutes.

Remove from heat and allow the pressure to drop naturally.

Transfer the beets to a bowl and let cool slightly then slip off the skins, discard the tops, and cut into cubes.

Return the beets to the soup, stir in the balsamic vinegar then simmer for 10 minutes.

Season to taste with salt, pepper and paprika then stir in the dill.

In a small bowl, whisk together the sour cream and flour and stir into the hot soup.

Cook, stirring for about 5 minutes or until hot (but not boiling) and slightly thickened.

Serve immediately.

Pumpkin Soup

Cooking time: 8 minutes
Serves 8

Start your next Thanksgiving meal with this classic seasonal soup. Use evaporated milk instead of cream to help keep the fat content low, but without compromising the creamy texture or taste.

Ingredients

1/4 cup (50 ml) butter
2 large onions, chopped
1 stalk celery, chopped
2 leeks, white parts only, chopped
3 large carrots, chopped
3 large potatoes, chopped
6 cups (1.5 L) vegetable stock
2 cups (500 ml) cubed peeled fresh pumpkin or canned pumpkin purée
1-1/2 cups (375 ml) whipping (35%) cream or evaporated milk
Salt and freshly ground black pepper to taste
2 tablespoons (25 ml) butter
1/4 cup (50 ml) chopped green onion
1/4 cup (50 ml) chopped parsley

Directions

In a pressure cooker, melt 1/4 cup (50 ml) butter over medium heat then add the onions and celery and sauté for 5 minutes.

Add the leeks, carrots and potatoes and cook, stirring, for another 5 minutes.

Stir in the stock and pumpkin.

Lock the lid in place and bring the cooker up to full pressure over high heat then reduce the heat to medium-low, just to maintain even pressure, and cook for 8 minutes.

Remove from heat and release the pressure quickly then let cool slightly

In a food processor, purée the solids with some of the cooking liquid until smooth then return the purée to the cooker and stir in the whipping cream.

Heat through but don't boil.

Season to taste with salt and pepper and whisk in the butter until melted.

Stir in the green onions and parsley.

Serve immediately.

Moroccan Harira Soup with Chickpeas

Cooking time: 20 minutes
Serves 4

The chili pepper gives this tomato-based soup a little zing. Choose a scotch bonnet pepper for a spicier version.

Ingredients

1/2 cup (125 ml) dried chickpeas
2 tablespoons (25 ml) olive oil
1 large onion, chopped
1 chopped jalapeno or scotch bonnet pepper (the latter is hotter)
1/2 cup (125 ml) chopped celery
1 teaspoon (5 ml) ground ginger
1 teaspoon (5 ml) ground turmeric
1/2 teaspoon (2 ml) ground cinnamon
1/2 teaspoon (2 ml) crumbled saffron (optional)
1/2 teaspoon (2 ml) freshly ground black pepper
4 cups (1 L) water
3 cups (750 ml) chopped tomatoes or 1 can (28 ounces [796 ml]) crushed tomatoes
1 can (10 ounces [284 ml]) vegetable broth
3/4 cup (175 ml) green or brown lentils
3 tablespoons (45 ml) lemon juice
Lemon slices for garnish

Directions

Soak the chickpeas overnight in water to cover or use the quick pressure-soak method* then drain.

In a pressure cooker, heat the oil over medium heat then add the onion, jalapeno and celery and sauté for about 5 minutes or until soft.

Stir in the ginger, turmeric, cinnamon, saffron, and pepper and cook for 1 minute until fragrant.

Stir in the chickpeas, water, tomatoes, broth, lentils, and lemon juice, making sure the cooker is no more than half full.

Lock the lid in place and bring the cooker up to full pressure over high heat then reduce the heat to medium-low, just to maintain even pressure, and cook for 20 minutes.

Remove from heat and allow the pressure to drop naturally.

Serve garnished with lemon slices.

*For further directions please refer to the Pressure Soaking instructions found in the "Introduction" section of this book.

Spicy Mixed Bean and Barley Soup

Cooking time: 20 minutes
Serves 6

This chunky vegetarian soup is perfect when you have a lot of different peas, beans and lentils to use up. Use the legumes called for in the recipe, or substitute whatever beans you have on hand.

Ingredients

1 cup (250 ml) mixed dried beans (red, white, black, pinto, black-eyed peas)
1/2 cup (125 ml) pearl or pot barley
1/4 cup (50 ml) green or yellow split peas
1/4 cup (50 ml) small red lentils
2 teaspoons (10 ml) ground cumin
2 teaspoons (10 ml) dried oregano
1 bay leaf
1 small dried chili pepper, crumbled, or 1/2 teaspoon (2 ml) red pepper flakes
1 teaspoon (5 ml) chili powder
5 cups (1.25 L) cold water
2 cloves garlic, minced
1 stalk celery, chopped
1 onion, minced
1 can (14 ounces [398 ml]) tomatoes, chopped
Salt and freshly ground black pepper to taste
2 tablespoons (25 ml) chopped parsley

Directions

Soak the beans overnight in water to cover or use the quick pressure-soak method* then drain.

In a pressure cooker, combine the beans, barley, split peas, lentils, cumin, oregano, bay leaf, chili pepper, chili powder, water, garlic, celery, onion and tomatoes.

Lock the lid in place and bring the cooker up to full pressure over high heat then reduce the heat to medium-low, just to maintain even pressure, and cook for 20 minutes.

Remove from heat and allow the pressure to drop naturally.

The beans and barley should be very tender. If not, lock the lid in place and bring to full pressure and cook for 5 minutes longer then allow the pressure to drop naturally.

Discard the bay leaf and season to taste with salt and pepper, then stir in the parsley.

*For further directions please refer to the Pressure Soaking instructions found on the introduction page.

Wild Mushroom and Potato Bisque

Cooking time: 5 minutes
Serves 4

There's very little cream in this elegant mushroom soup. It gets its smooth texture from potatoes. To speed things up even more, use the food processor to mince the vegetables and mushrooms.

Ingredients

1 tablespoon (15 ml) olive oil
2 cloves garlic, minced
1 small onion, minced
1 small tomato, seeded and chopped
1 cup (250 ml) finely chopped wild and domestic mushrooms (brown, oyster, shiitake, Portobello, morels, cepes, etc.)
12 ounces (375 g) Yukon Gold potatoes (or other yellow-fleshed variety) peeled and grated
4 cups (1 L) vegetable stock
1 bay leaf
3/4 teaspoon (4 ml) minced thyme
1/2 cup (125 ml) whipping (35%) cream
Salt and freshly ground black pepper, to taste

Directions

In a pressure cooker, heat the oil over medium heat then add the garlic and onion and sauté for about 5 minutes or until soft.

Add the tomato, mushrooms and potatoes and cook, stirring, for about 5 minutes longer or until the mushrooms begin to give up their moisture.

Stir in the stock, bay leaf and thyme.

Lock the lid in place and bring the cooker up to full pressure over high heat, then reduce the heat to medium-low, just to maintain even pressure, and cook for 5 minutes.

Release the pressure quickly.

Discard the bay leaf then stir in the cream and heat through.

Using a potato masher, break up the potatoes to thicken the soup, if necessary, or use an immersion blender to purée if you prefer a smoother soup.

Season to taste with salt and pepper.

Spicy Sweet Potato Soup

Cooking time: 12 minutes
Serves 4

This soup is creamy, rich and smooth with hardly any added fat. The gorgeous orange color makes it the perfect prelude to a fall supper.

Ingredients

1 tablespoons (15 ml) olive oil
2 cloves garlic, minced
1 onion, chopped
3 cups (750 ml) vegetable stock
2 cups (500 ml) chopped peeled sweet potatoes
1 small potato, peeled and chopped
2 carrots, chopped
1 ancho chili, stem and seeds removed
1-1/2 teaspoon (7 ml) garam masala
Salt to taste

Directions

In a pressure cooker, heat the oil over medium heat then add the garlic and onion and sauté for 5 minutes or until soft.

Stir in the stock, sweet potatoes, potato, carrots and ancho chili.

Lock the lid in place and bring the cooker up to full pressure over high heat then reduce the heat to medium-low, just to maintain even pressure, and cook for 12 minutes.

Remove from heat and release the pressure quickly.

Purée the soup with an immersion blender or in a food processor until creamy and smooth then stir in the garam masala and season with salt to taste.

Winter Mushroom and Barley Soup

Cooking time: 20 minutes
Serves 6

There's nothing delicate about this vegetarian soup – the Portobello mushrooms and barley provide plenty of hearty flavor.

Ingredients

2 tablespoons (25 ml) butter
1 tablespoon (15 ml) olive oil
1 large onion, halved and sliced
2 stalks celery, chopped
1 carrot, chopped
2 teaspoons (10 ml) minced garlic
1 bay leaf
1 Portobello mushrooms cap, chopped
8 ounces (250 g) mixed fresh mushrooms, sliced
1/2 cup (125 ml) pearl or pot barley
6 cups (1.5 L) water
2 tablespoons (25 ml) vermouth or brandy
2 teaspoons (10 ml) salt
1/4 teaspoon (1 ml) freshly ground black pepper
Chopped parsley to garnish

Directions

In a pressure cooker, heat the butter and oil over medium heat then add the onion and sauté for 5 minutes or until softened.

Stir in the celery, carrot, garlic, and bay leaf and cook, stirring, for 10 minutes or until the onion begins to turn golden.

Add the Portobello and mixed mushrooms and cook for 5 minutes, until they release their moisture.

Stir in the barley, water, vermouth, salt and pepper.

Lock the lid in place and bring the cooker up to full pressure over high heat then reduce the heat to medium-low, just to maintain even pressure, and cook for 20 minutes.

Remove from heat and allow the pressure to drop naturally.

Discard the bay leaf and adjust the seasoning with salt and pepper to taste.

Serve immediately, sprinkled with parsley.

Entrees and Salads

THE RECIPES

~ 45 ~

Warm Lemon Lentil Salad

Cooking time: 8 minutes
Serves 4 to 6

Lentil salad is a traditional French first course. Use the regular brown or green lentils in this dish or the smaller French green lentils if you can find them.

Ingredients

1 sprig thyme
1 sprig rosemary
1 bay leaf
1 cup (250 ml) brown or green lentils
2 cloves garlic, peeled
1 carrot, quartered
3 cups (750 ml) water
1 tablespoon (15 ml) vegetable oil

Dressing

Zest of 1 lemon, minced
Juice of 1 lemon (about 3 tablespoons [45 ml] juice)
2 teaspoons (10 ml) chopped thyme (or 1 teaspoon [5 ml]) dried)
1 clove garlic, minced
1 teaspoon (5 ml) salt
1 tablespoon (15 ml) Dijon mustard
1/4 cup (50 ml) extra virgin olive oil
Freshly ground black pepper
4 plum tomatoes, seeded and chopped
3 green onions, chopped
1/4 cup (50 ml) chopped parsley
Mixed greens

Directions

Using kitchen string, tie the thyme, rosemary and bay leaf into a bundle.

In a pressure cooker, combine the herb bundle, lentils, garlic, carrot, water and oil.

Lock the lid in place and bring the cooker up to full pressure over high heat then reduce the heat to medium-low, just to maintain even pressure, and cook for 8 minutes.

Remove from heat and allow the pressure to drop naturally then drain well.

Discard the herb bundle, carrot and garlic and transfer the lentils to a bowl.

Dressing

In a bowl, whisk together the lemon zest, lemon juice, thyme, garlic, salt and mustard then slowly whisk in the olive oil to emulsify.

Season with the pepper to taste.

Pour the dressing over the lentils and toss to coat.

Stir in the tomatoes, green onions and parsley.

Serve the salad warm over the mixed greens or as a base for grilled meat or fish.

Braised Greens

Cooking time: 10 minutes
Serves 4

Use Swiss chard, beet greens, turnip greens or spinach in this healthy combination, inspired by the wild "horta" served in the mountains of Greece. Make sure to include some bitter greens like dandelion or endive.

Ingredients

1-1/2 pounds (750 g) mixed greens (chard, spinach, beet greens, dandelion greens, endives, etc...)
3 cloves garlic, minced
2 cups (500 ml) water
1 teaspoon (5 ml) salt
1 teaspoon (5 ml) vinegar
1/4 cup (50 ml) good quality peppery olive oil
1 lemon, cut into wedges

Directions

Wash the greens well to remove any grit then remove the woody stems and discard.

Roll the leafy greens into cigar-like tubes and slice into strips.

In a pressure cooker, combine the greens, garlic, water, salt and vinegar.

Lock the lid in place and bring up to full pressure over high heat then reduce the heat to medium, just to maintain pressure, and steam for 10 minutes.

Reduce the pressure quickly and remove the lid.

Drain the excess liquid from the greens if desired, or serve in deep bowls with the juices.

Drizzle with olive oil and squeeze fresh lemon juice over each serving.

Chickpea Salad with Roasted Onions and Bell Peppers

Cooking time: 15 minutes
Serves 4

This flavorful and healthy salad is ideal for taking to a picnic or to carry on a hike. The salad is delicious on the day you make it, but just as good the next day. You'll be amazed how toothsome and delicious chickpeas can be when cooked from scratch in the pressure cooker.

Ingredients

1 cup (250 ml) dried chickpeas
4 cups (1 L) water
1 red bell pepper
2 teaspoon (10 ml) olive oil
1 large onion
1 head garlic
2 plum tomatoes, seeded and chopped
1 tablespoon (15 ml) chopped thyme (or 1 teaspoon [5 ml] dried)
1 tablespoon (15 ml) chopped sage leaves (or 1 teaspoon [5 ml] dried)
1 teaspoon (5 ml) sea salt
1/2 teaspoon (2 ml) freshly ground black pepper
1/2 teaspoon (2 ml) cayenne pepper
1/4 cup (50 ml) extra virgin olive oil
3 tablespoons (45 ml) lemon juice
1/4 cup (50 ml) minced Italian parsley

Directions

Soak the chickpeas overnight in water to cover or use the quick pressure-soak method* then drain.

In a pressure cooker, combine the chickpeas and water.

Lock the lid in place and bring the cooker up to full pressure over high heat then reduce the heat to medium-low, just to maintain even pressure, and cook for 15 minutes.

Remove from heat and allow the pressure to drop naturally then drain.

Transfer to a large bowl.

Meanwhile, on the barbecue or under the broiler, char the red pepper then place in a bag to cool.

Peel of the skin from the pepper, remove the seeds, chop then add to the chickpeas in the bowl.

Wrap the onion and garlic, unpeeled, in a piece of foil and drizzle with olive oil then roast in a preheated 400°F (200°C) oven for 45 minutes or until very soft.

Peel the onion and cut into slivers and add to the chickpeas in the bowl.

Squeeze the garlic out of the skins into the bowl.

Add the tomatoes, thyme, sage, salt, pepper, cayenne, olive oil and lemon juice and toss to coat.

Cool to room temperature and let stand for 1 hour to allow the flavors to meld.

Just before serving, stir in the parsley.

*For further directions please refer to the Pressure Soaking instructions found in the "Introduction" section of this book.

Barley Risotto Primavera

Cooking time: 18 minutes
Serves 6

This dish is just like the famous Italian specialty, but made with whole barley for a unique prairie twist.

Ingredients

2 tablespoons (25 ml) olive oil
1 cup (250 ml) pearl or pot barley
1 small onion, minced
1 clove garlic, minced
1/2 cup (125 ml) finely chopped zucchini
1/4 cup (50 ml) minced carrot
1/4 cup (50 ml) minced celery
2-1/2 cup (625 ml) vegetable stock or water
1 teaspoon (5 ml) tamari soy sauce
1/4 cup (50 ml) freshly grated Parmesan cheese
1/8 teaspoon (0.5 ml) freshly ground black pepper

Directions

In a pressure cooker, heat the oil over medium heat then add the barley and sauté for 1 minute or until toasted.

Add the onion, garlic, zucchini, carrot and celery and sauté for 1 minute longer or until the vegetables begin to soften.

Stir in the stock and soy sauce.

Lock the lid in place and bring the cooker up to full pressure over high heat then reduce the heat to medium-low, just to maintain even pressure, and cook for 18 minutes.

Remove from heat and allow the pressure to drop naturally.

Fluff the risotto with a spoon then stir in the Parmesan cheese and pepper.

Serve immediately.

Chestnuts with Red Cabbage and Apples

Cooking time: 10 minutes
Serves 4 to 6

This dish is a nice holiday alternative to the usual Brussels sprouts. Despite their rich flavor, chestnuts are actually low in fat.

Ingredients

2 tablespoons (25 ml) butter
1 onion, chopped
1 pound (500 g) shredded red cabbage
2 green apples, peeled and cut into wedges
1 cup (250 ml) peeled fresh chestnuts or rehydrated dried chestnuts *
1 teaspoon (5 ml) salt
1/2 cup (125 ml) dry white wine
1/2 cup (125 ml) water or vegetable stock
1/4 teaspoon (1 ml) freshly ground black pepper

Directions

In a pressure cooker, melt the butter over medium heat then add the onions and sauté for 5 minutes or until softened.

Add the cabbage, stirring to coat with the butter then add the apples, chestnuts, salt, wine and water.

Lock the lid in place and bring the cooker up to full pressure over high heat then reduce the heat to medium-low, just to maintain even pressure, and cook for 10 minutes.

Remove from heat and release the pressure quickly.

Simmer, uncovered, until the liquid is reduced.

Stir in the pepper and serve immediately.

* *Tip:* The pressure cooked makes peeling chestnuts fast and easy. Cut an X in the base of each nut and place in the cooker. Cook the nuts with plenty of water, lock the lid in place and cook at high pressure for 6 minutes. You will find it is easy to peel of the shells and the brown, papery skin (which is bitter).

Chickpeas and Mixed Vegetable Stew

Cooking time: 19 minutes
Serves 8

This substantial stew provides a gardenful of healthy vegetables in one pot. Here's proof positive that vegetarian food can be hearty enough for the coldest winter day.

Ingredients

1 cup (250 ml) dried chickpeas
4 cups (1 L) water
2 tablespoons (25 ml) olive oil
3 cloves garlic, minced
2 stalks celery, chopped
1 onion, chopped
2 large potatoes, peeled and chopped
1 red bell pepper, chopped
1 large carrot, chopped
1/2 cup (125 ml) small red lentils
2 cups (500 ml) vegetable stock
1/2 cup (125 ml) dry white wine
3 tablespoons (45 ml) chopped basil or basil pesto
1 tablespoon (15 ml) chopped rosemary
Salt and freshly ground black pepper to taste
2 cups (500 ml) polenta, cooked
Extra virgin olive oil for drizzling
1/2 cup (125 ml) freshly grated Parmesan cheese

Directions

Soak the chickpeas overnight in water to cover or use the quick pressure-soak method* then drain.

In a pressure cooker, combine the chickpeas and water then lock the lid in place and bring the cooker up to full pressure over high heat. Reduce the heat to medium-low, just to maintain even pressure, and cook for 14 minutes.

Remove from heat and allow the pressure to drop naturally then drain and set aside.

Wipe the cooker clean then add the oil and heat over medium heat.

Add the garlic, celery and onion and sauté until the onion is soft.

Add the potatoes, red pepper, and carrot then toss to coat with oil.

Add the chickpeas, lentils, stock and wine.

Lock the lid in place and bring the cooker up to full pressure over high heat then reduce the heat to medium-low, just to maintain even pressure, and cook for 5 minutes.

Remove from heat and allow the pressure to drop naturally.

Stir in the basil and rosemary then heat, uncovered, over low heat for 5 minutes and season to taste with salt and pepper.

Serve the stew in deep bowls over a mound of soft polenta, drizzle with extra virgin olive oil and sprinkle with Parmesan.

*For further directions please refer to the Pressure Soaking instructions found in the "Introduction" section of this book.

Polenta

Ingredients

8 cups (2 L) water
2 cups (500 ml) coarsely ground cornmeal
4 tablespoons (50 ml) butter
1/2 cup (125 ml) finely grated Parmesan cheese

Directions

In a large heavy-bottomed saucepan, bring the water to a boil then reduce the heat to low and add the cornmeal in a slow, thin stream, whisking constantly.

With a wooden spoon, stir every minute or so until the mixture pulls away from the side of the pan in one mass. (Depending on coarseness of cornmeal, this will take from 5 to 20 minutes.)

Stir in the butter and cheese.

Vegetable Couscous

Cooking time: 18 minutes
Serves 4

Couscous is one of those wonderful accompaniments that add interest to everyday meals without a lot of fuss. This is an almost-instant vegetarian meal in a pot, featuring plenty of healthy vegetables and exotic Moroccan flavors.

Ingredients

1 cup (250 ml) dried chickpeas
4 cups (1 L) cold water
2 tablespoons (25 ml) olive oil
1 onion, chopped
1 clove garlic, minced
1 red or yellow bell pepper, chopped
2 teaspoons (10 ml) ground cumin
1 teaspoon (5 ml) Hungarian paprika
1/2 teaspoon (2 ml) salt
1/4 teaspoon (1 ml) freshly ground black pepper
1/4 teaspoon (1 ml) ground cinnamon
1/8 teaspoon (0.5 ml) cayenne pepper
1/4 cup (50 ml) currants or raisins
2 cups (500 ml) vegetable stock
1-1/2 cups (325 ml) couscous
1 small zucchini, diced
1 cup (250 ml) frozen green peas, thawed
3 tablespoons (45 ml) chopped fresh cilantro

Directions

Soak the chickpeas overnight in water to cover or use the quick pressure-soak method* then drain.

In a pressure cooker, combine the chickpeas with the water then lock the lid in place and bring the cooker to full pressure over high heat. Reduce the heat to medium-low, just to maintain even pressure, and cook for 14 minutes.

Remove from heat and allow the pressure to drop naturally then drain and set aside.

Wipe the cooker clean then add the oil and heat over medium heat.

Add the onions, garlic and bell pepper and sauté for 5 minutes or until softened.

Stir in the cumin, paprika, salt, pepper, cinnamon and cayenne and cook for 2 minutes longer.

Stir in the chickpeas and raisins then pour in the stock.

Lock the lid in place and bring the cooker up to full pressure over high heat then reduce the heat to medium-low, just to maintain even pressure, and cook for 4 minutes.

Remove from heat and release the pressure quickly.

Stir in the couscous, zucchini and peas then let stand covered for 10 minutes.

Fluff with a fork and stir in the cilantro.

*For further directions please refer to the Pressure Soaking instructions found in the "Introduction" section of the book.

Warm Gigandes Bean Salad

Cooking time: 12 minutes
Serves 6

I discovered these giant white beans while on a trip to Greece. Use any large white bean, but try to find an heirloom variety like these meaty white beans, which are as big as your thumb and are usually available at Greek or Mediterranean groceries. Serve as a started salad over sturdy mixed greens, such as romaine, curly chicory and arugula.

Ingredients

1 cup (250 ml) dry gigandes beans
2 roma tomatoes, seeded and finely chopped
1/3 cup (75 ml) air-cured black olives, seeded and chopped
1/4 cup (50 ml) extra-virgin olive oil (preferably Greek)
Zest and juice of 1/2 lemon (about 1 teaspoon/5 ml minced zest and 2 tablespoons/25 ml juice)
2 tablespoons (25 ml) basil pesto (homemade or commercial)
Salt and freshly ground black pepper

Directions

Soak the beans overnight in plenty of cold water or use the quick pressure soak method*.

Drain the beans and place them in the pressure cooker then add enough cold water to cover them by 2 to 3-inches.

Lock the lid in place and bring the cooker up to high pressure over high heat and cook for 12 minutes.

Allow the pressure to drop naturally (this helps to keep the beans intact) then drain the beans well.

While the beans are cooking, combine the chopped tomatoes, olives, olive oil, lemon zest and juice in a bowl then stir in the warm beans and pesto.

Season to taste with salt and pepper.

* To speed up the soaking process, you can place the beans in water in a pot and bring them to a full, rolling boil. Simmer the beans for 2 minutes, then remove the pot from the heat, cover it, and let the beans soak for 1 hour. Drain away those gaseous complex carbs and proceed with your recipe.

Biryani

Cooking time: 7 minutes
Serves 2 as a main dish or 4 as a side dish

You can add almost any vegetable to this wonderful Indian rice dish.

Ingredients

2 tablespoons (25 ml) vegetable oil
2 teaspoons (10 ml) salt
2 teaspoons (10 ml) sweet Spanish or Hungarian paprika
2 teaspoons (10 ml) turmeric
2 teaspoons (10 ml) garam masala
1/2 teaspoon (2 ml) cayenne pepper
1 onion, halved and sliced
1/2 cup (125 ml) small mushrooms, halved
Half a green pepper, diced
1 cup (250 ml) basmati rice
1/2 cup (125 ml) small florets cauliflower
1/2 cup (125 ml) diced carrots
1/4 cup (50 ml) chopped dried apricots or raisins
2 cups (500 ml) water or vegetable stock
1/2 cup (125 ml) frozen peas, thawed

Directions

In a pressure cooker, heat the oil over low heat then add the salt, paprika, turmeric, garam masala and cayenne and cook, stirring, for 1 minute.

Increase heat to medium and add the onion, mushrooms, and green pepper and sauté for 2 to 3 minutes or until the mushrooms begin to give up their liquid.

Stir in the rice, cauliflower, carrots, and apricots then pour in the water.

Lock the lid in place and bring the cooker up to full pressure over high heat then reduce the heat to medium-low, just to maintain even pressure, and cook for 7 minutes.

Remove from heat and allow the pressure to drop naturally for 2 minutes then release the remaining pressure quickly.

Stir in the peas then replace the cover on the cooker (but do not lock) and let steam for 5 minutes.

Fluff with a fork.

Caribbean Red Bean and Barley

Cooking time: 10 minutes, plus 7 minutes for pearl barley or 15 minutes for hulled barley
Serves 6 to 8

Here's a flavorful combination of Canadian beans and barley, with a burst of Island heat.

Ingredients

1 cup (250 ml) dried red kidney beans
2 cloves garlic, minced
2 stalks celery, chopped
1 small onion, chopped
4 cups (1 L) water
1-1/2 cups (375 ml) pearl or hulled barley
1 whole scotch bonnet pepper or 2 whole jalapeno peppers
2 teaspoons (10 ml) dried thyme
2 cups (500 ml) unsweetened coconut milk
3 green onions, minced
1 tablespoon (15 ml) butter
Salt and white pepper to taste

Directions

Soak the beans overnight in water to cover or use the quick pressure-soak method* then drain.

In a pressure cooker, combine the beans, garlic, celery, onion and water.

Lock the lid in place and bring the cooker up to full pressure over high heat then reduce the heat to medium-low, just to maintain even pressure, and cook for 10 minutes.

Remove from heat and allow the pressure to drop naturally.

Stir in the barley, scotch bonnet pepper, thyme and coconut milk.

Lock the lid in place and bring the cooker up to full pressure over high heat then reduce the heat to medium-low, just to maintain even pressure, and cook or 7 minutes for pearl barley or 15 minutes for hulled barley.

Remove from heat and allow the pressure to drop naturally.

Discard the scotch bonnet pepper then stir in the green onions and butter.

Season to taste with salt and white pepper and serve immediately.

* For further directions please refer to the Pressure Soaking instructions found in the "Introduction" section of this book.

Creamy Lentils and Cheddar

Cooking time: 10 minutes
Serves 4

This vegetarian dish is simple and homey – your high-fiber alternative to mac and cheese.

Ingredients

2 cloves garlic, minced
1 cup (250 ml) brown or green lentils
1 cup (250 ml) chopped onion
1 carrot, grated
1 yellow or red bell pepper, minced
1 bay leaf
1/2 (2 ml) teaspoon dried thyme
1 can (14 ounces [398 ml]) tomatoes, puréed
1 cup (250 ml) water
1/2 cup (125 ml) whipping (35%) cream
1 cup (250 ml) grated old Cheddar cheese

Directions

In a pressure cooker, combine the garlic, lentils, onions, carrot, pepper, bay leaf, thyme, tomatoes, and water. (Make sure the cooker is no more than half full.)

Lock the lid in place and bring the cooker up to full pressure over high heat then reduce the heat to medium-low, just to maintain even pressure, and cook for 10 minutes.

Remove from heat and allow the pressure to drop naturally.

The lentils should be tender. If not, return to full pressure and cook for 2 to 4 minutes longer. Remove from heat and allow the pressure to drop naturally.

Discard the bay leaf, stir in the cream and bring to a boil then reduce the heat and simmer until the sauce is thickened.

Remove from heat and add the cheese and stir gently until the cheese is melted and combined.

Boston "Baked" Beans

Cooking time: 6 minutes for navy beans or 10 minutes for Great
Northern beans plus 2 minutes
Serves 6

Ingredients

3 cups (750 ml) dried white navy beans or Great Northern beans
6-1/2 cups (1.625 L) water, divided
2 cloves garlic, minced
1 cup (250 ml) chopped onions
1/4 cup (50 ml) packed brown sugar
1/4 teaspoon (1 ml) freshly ground black pepper
1 cup (250 ml) tomato sauce
2 tablespoons (25 ml) olive oil
1/4 cup (50 ml) molasses
2 tablespoons (25 ml) Dijon mustard
1 to 2 teaspoons (5 to 10 ml) salt (or to taste)

Directions

Soak the beans overnight in water to cover or use the quick pressure-
soak method* then drain.

In a pressure cooker, combine the beans with 6 cups (1.5 L) of the
water.

Lock the lid in place and bring the cooker up to full pressure over high
heat then reduce the heat to medium-low, just to maintain even
pressure, and cook for 6 minutes for navy beans or 10 minutes for
Great Northern beans.

Remove from heat and allow the pressure to drop naturally then drain.

Whisk the remaining water into the cooker, together with the garlic,
onion, brown sugar, pepper, tomato sauce, oil, molasses and mustard
then stir in the beans.

Lock the lid in place and bring the cooker up to full pressure over high heat then reduce the heat to medium-low, just to maintain even pressure and cook for 2 minutes.

Remove from heat and allow the pressure to drop naturally.

The beans should be tender. If not, add a little water (if necessary) and lock the lid in place. Return to full pressure and cook for 2 to 3 minutes longer. Remove from heat and allow the pressure to drop naturally.

Drain off any excess liquid or let the beans sit, covered, for 30 minutes until more of the liquid is absorbed.

Season to taste with salt.

* For further directions please refer to the Pressure Soaking instructions found in the "Introduction" section of this book.

Vegetarian Barley, Lentil and Black Bean Chili

Cooking time: 10 minutes
Serves 6

Here's a great alternative to traditional meat-based chili. The beans, lentils and grains combine to form a complete protein – plus a chewy, meaty texture that will satisfy any carnivore.

Ingredients

2 tablespoons (25 ml) vegetable oil
3 cloves garlic, minced
1 large Spanish onion, chopped
1 jalapeno, scotch bonnet or serrano chili, seeded and minced
1 cup (250 ml) brown or green lentils
1 cup (250 ml) cooked black beans
1 cup (250 ml) pearl barley
3 tablespoons (45 ml) chili powder
1 tablespoons (15 ml) sweet Hungarian paprika
1 teaspoon (5 ml) dried oregano
1 teaspoon (5 ml) ground cumin
6 cups (1.5 L) vegetable stock
1 chipotle pepper in adobo sauce, chopped
1 can (28 ounces [796 ml]) plum tomatoes, crushed
Salt and freshly ground black pepper, to taste

Directions

In a pressure cooker, heat the oil over medium heat then add the garlic and onion and sauté until tender.

Add the chili pepper and sauté for 1 minute then stir in the lentils, black beans, barley, chili powder, paprika, oregano, cumin, stock, chipotle pepper and tomatoes.

Lock the lid in place and bring the cooker up to full pressure over high heat then reduce the heat to medium-low, just to maintain even pressure, and cook for 10 minutes.

Remove from heat and allow the pressure to drop naturally for 10 minutes then release any remaining pressure quickly.

The barley and lentils should be tender. If not, return to full pressure for 2 to 3 minutes longer then remove from the heat and allow the pressure to drop naturally.

Simmer, uncovered, until thickened then season to taste with salt and pepper.

Curried Lentils with Spinach

Cooking time: 12 minutes
Serves 4

With a pressure cooker, this classic Indian dish is ready in a fraction of the time normally required to prepare it. Serve as a side dish with an Indian meal, or simply over a pile of Basmati rice.

Ingredients

2 tablespoons (25 ml) vegetable oil
2 dried hot peppers, crushed
1/2 teaspoon (2 ml) cumin seeds
1/2 teaspoon (2 ml) ground coriander
1/2 teaspoon (2 ml) mustard seed or dried mustard
2 cloves garlic, minced
1 onion, minced
1 large tomato, seeded and chopped
1 tablespoon (15 ml) minced ginger root
1 cup (250 ml) brown or green lentils
1/2 teaspoon (2 ml) salt
3-1/2 cups (875 ml) water
2 tablespoons (25 ml) lemon juice
2 cups (250 ml) fresh spinach, washed thoroughly and finely chopped
(or 1 package frozen chopped spinach, thawed and squeezed dry)
Coriander chutney or mango chutney as a condiment

Directions

In a pressure cooker, heat the oil over medium heat then add the hot peppers, cumin seed, coriander and mustard seed and sauté for about 20 seconds or until fragrant.

Add the garlic, onion, tomato and ginger and sauté for 3 minutes or until the vegetables are soft and the tomato begins to break down.

Stir in the lentils, salt, water, lemon juice, and spinach.

Lock the lid in place and bring the cooker up to full pressure over high heat then reduce the heat to medium-low, just to maintain even pressure, and cook for 12 minutes.

Remove from heat and allow the pressure to drop naturally.

Simmer uncovered to reduce the liquid if necessary.

Serve over basmati rice with a dollop of coriander or mango chutney on the side.

Spanish Potatoes and Chickpeas

Cooking time: 18 minutes
Serves 4 as a main course of 8 to 10 for tapas

With its rich, garlicky saffron sauce, this dish is the ultimate vegetarian comfort food. Serve it in little bowls with crusty bread for a hot tapas starter, as an everyday main course, or as an exotic side dish.

Ingredients

1 cup (250 ml) dried chickpeas
1/4 cup (50 ml) olive oil
4 Yukon gold potatoes (or other yellow-fleshed variety), peeled and cut into 1-inch (2.5 cm) cubes
2 onions, chopped
5 large cloves garlic, minced
1/2 teaspoon (2 ml) saffron threads
3 bay leaves
3 cups (750 ml) vegetable stock or water
1 tablespoons (15 ml) sweet Spanish paprika
1-1/2 cup (375 ml) quartered artichoke hearts (1 can 14 ounces [398 ml])
Salt and freshly ground black pepper
3 tablespoons (45 ml) fresh parsley
Shaved Parmesan (optional)
Lemon wedges (optional)

Directions

Soak the chickpeas overnight in water to cover or use the quick pressure-soak method* then drain.

In a pressure cooker, heat the oil over medium heat then add the potatoes and onions and sauté until the onions are tender.

Add the garlic and saffron and sauté for 1 minute then stir in the chickpeas, bay leaves and stock.

Lock the lid in place and bring the cooker up to full pressure over high heat then reduce the heat to medium-low, just to maintain even pressure, and cook for 18 minutes.

Remove from heat and release the pressure quickly.

Discard the bay leaves then stir in the paprika and artichoke hearts and simmer uncovered over medium heat, breaking up some of the potatoes, until the stew is nicely thickened.

Season to taste with salt and pepper then stir in the parsley.

If desired, serve with shaved Parmesan and lemon wedges to squeeze over top.

* For further directions please refer to the Pressure Soaking instructions found in the "Introduction" section of the book.

Beans and Grains

THE RECIPES

Black Bean Chili

Cooking time: 20 minutes
Serves 6 to 8

With earthy black beans, smoky chipotle chilies and a good shot of prairie rye whiskey, this is truly an outstanding vegetarian bean dish. Serve it over rice or rolled up in flour tortillas with chopped tomatoes and grated cheese.

Ingredients

2 cups (500 ml) dried black turtle beans
3 tablespoons (45 ml) vegetable oil
1 large onion, chopped
2 tablespoons (25 ml) paprika
1 tablespoon (15 ml) dried oregano
2 teaspoons (10 ml) cumin seed
1/4 teaspoon (1 ml) cayenne pepper
2 cloves garlic, minced
1 chipotle chili in adobo sauce, chopped or 1 rehydrated dried chipotle, chopped
1 green pepper, chopped
1 can (28 ounces [796 ml]) plum tomatoes, chopped
1 bay leaf
1 cup (250 ml) water
1/2 cup (125 ml) rye whiskey
2 teaspoons (10 ml) salt, or to taste
1/2 cup (125 ml) chopped cilantro
1 cup (250 ml) grated Cheddar cheese
1 cup (250 ml) sour cream (preferably a low-fat variety)

Directions

Soak the beans overnight in water to cover or use the quick pressure-soak method* then drain.

In a pressure cooker, heat the oil over medium heat then add the onion and sauté for 5 minutes or until just starting to brown.

Add the paprika, oregano, cumin and cayenne and cook, stirring constantly, for 2 minutes or just until the spices are fragrant.

Add the garlic, chipotle, green pepper and tomatoes then stir in the beans, bay leaf, water and rye whiskey.

Lock the lid in place and bring the cooker up to full pressure then reduce the heat to medium-low, just to maintain even pressure, and cook for 20 minutes.

Remove from heat and allow the pressure to drop naturally.

The beans should be tender. If not, return to full pressure and cook for 2 to 3 minutes longer. Remove from heat and allow the pressure to drop naturally.

If the beans are too soupy, simmer, uncovered, until reduced and thickened. Alternatively, transfer 1/2 cup (125 ml) of the beans to a bowl or food processor and mash or purée and stir into the pot.

Discard the bay leaf and season to taste with salt and stir in the cilantro.

Serve over a mound of fluffy rice, topped with a sprinkling of grated cheese and a dollop of sour cream.

* For further directions please refer to the Pressure Soaking instructions found in the "Introduction" section of this book.

Basic Risotto

Cooking time: 7 minutes
Serves 4 as a side dish

The pressure cooker makes cooking creamy risotto so easy, you'll be serving it instead of regular rice all the time. The saffron is optional, but it gives the risotto a wonderful earthy flavor and golden color. A wood rasp makes an excellent grater for the Parmesan.

Ingredients

1 tablespoon (15 ml) butter
1 tablespoon (15 ml) olive oil
1 small onion, minced
1 cup (250 ml) Arborio rice or other short-grain rice
1/4 cup (50 ml) dry white wine
2 cups (500 ml) vegetable stock
1/2 teaspoon (2 ml) crushed saffron threads (optional)
1/2 cup (125 ml) freshly grated Parmesan cheese
Freshly ground black pepper

Directions

In a pressure cooker heat the butter and oil over medium heat then add the onion and sauté for 5 minutes or until soft (but not brown).

Stir in the rice, coating well with oil then add the wine.

If using, crumble the saffron into the stock and pour the stock over the rice.

Lock the lid in place and bring the cooker up to full pressure over high heat then reduce the heat to medium-low, just to maintain even pressure, and cook for 7 minutes.

Remove from heat and release the pressure quickly.

Stir in the Parmesan cheese and season to taste with pepper.

Serve immediately.

Risotto with Grilled Vegetables and Beet Greens

Cooking time: 7 minutes
Serves 4

Loaded with grilled vegetables and healthy greens, this risotto may be served as a vegetarian main course.

Ingredients

1/4 cup (50 ml) extra virgin olive oil
1 clove garlic, minced
1 small Asian eggplant, sliced
1 small zucchini, sliced
1 Portobello mushroom, stem removed
1 red or yellow bell pepper, seeded and halved
1 onion, thickly sliced
Salt and freshly ground black pepper to taste
1/4 cup (50 ml) butter, divided
1 cup (250 ml) Arborio rice or other short-grain rice
1/2 cup (125 ml) dry white wine
2 cups (500 ml) vegetable stock
2 cups (500 ml) slivered young beet greens
1/4 cup (50 ml) slivered basil leaves
1/2 cup (125 ml) freshly grated Parmesan cheese

Directions

In a small bowl, combine the oil and garlic and let stand at room temperature for 10 minutes to infuse the flavor.

Brush the garlic oil mixture over the eggplant, zucchini, mushroom, bell pepper, and onion then season with salt and pepper.

Grill over medium heat, turning once, until softened and slightly charred then let cool.

Chop coarsely and set aside.

In a pressure cooked, heat 3 tablespoons (45 ml) of the butter with any of the remaining oil and garlic over medium heat then add the rice, stirring to coat.

Stir in the wine and stock.

Lock the lid in place and bring the cooker up to full pressure over high heat then reduce the heat to medium-low, just to maintain even pressure, and cook for 7 minutes.

Remove from heat and release the pressure quickly.

Stir in the grilled vegetables, beet greens and basil then cover (but do not lock) and let stand just until the greens are wilted, about 5 minutes.

Stir in the Parmesan cheese and remaining butter and season to taste with pepper.

Roasted Garlic Risotto with Asiago

Cooking time: 7 minutes
Serves 4 to 6

Roasting tames the natural harshness of garlic and gives it a buttery, nutty flavor that works perfectly with the strong cheese in this dish. The lemon zest adds sparkle; the green onion, a touch of color. There's nothing complicated about this risotto, and it demonstrates once again just how easy it is to make a spectacular side dish in 7 short minutes.

Ingredients

1 head garlic
1 teaspoon (5 ml) olive oil
3 tablespoons (45 ml) butter
1 large onion, finely chopped
2 cups (500 ml) Arborio rice or other short-grain rice
1/2 cup (125 ml) dry white wine
4 cups (1 L) vegetable stock
1 cup (250 ml) freshly grated Asiago cheese
1/4 cup (50 ml) minced green onions
1 teaspoon (5 ml) minced lemon zest
Freshly ground black pepper to taste

Directions

To roast the garlic, cut the top quarter-inch form the whole head to expose the cloves and drizzle with oil and wrap loosely in foil.

Roast the garlic in a preheated oven for 30 to 40 minutes, or until the garlic is very soft then press the roasted garlic out of the skins and mash with the flat side of a knife and set aside.

In a pressure cooker, heat the butter over medium heat then add the onion and sauté for 5 minutes, until soft (but not brown).

Add the rice, stirring to coat then stir in the wine and cook until it has been absorbed.

Stir in the reserved garlic and vegetable broth.

Lock the lid in place and bring the cooker up to full pressure over high heat then reduce the heat to medium-low, just to maintain even pressure, and cook for 7 minutes.

Remove from heat and release the pressure quickly.

Stir in the cheese, green onions and lemon zest then season to taste with pepper.

Serve immediately.

Barley with Mint and Root Vegetables

Cooking time: 20 minutes
Serves 6

Barley is a healthy whole grain that makes a nice substitute for rice. Prepared in the pressure cooker, it's fast, toothsome and never sticky. Adding grated Parmesan to this dish gives it a flavor that's reminiscent of risotto.

Ingredients

1/4 cup (50 ml) butter
2 carrots, cut into small cubes
2 parsnips, cut into small cubes
1 sweet potato, peeled and cubed
1 onion, chopped
1 cup (250 ml) pot or pearl barley
3 cloves garlic, minced
3 cups (750 ml) vegetable stock
2 tablespoons (25 ml) chopped mint
2 tablespoons (25 ml) chopped parsley (optional)
1 cup (250 ml) finely grated Parmesan or Asiago cheese (optional)
Salt and freshly ground black pepper to taste

Directions

In a pressure cooker, heat the butter over medium heat then add the carrots, parsnips, sweet potato and onion and sauté until the vegetables start to caramelize.

Add the barley and garlic and cook, stirring for 5 minutes to toast the grains then pour in the stock.

Lock the lid in place and bring the cooker up to full pressure over high heat then reduce the heat to medium-low, just to maintain even pressure, and cook for 20 minutes.

Remove from heat and release the pressure quickly.

The barley should be tender. If not, cover (but do not lock) and simmer over low heat until tender.

Stir in the mint, parsley, and Parmesan (if using).

Season to taste with salt and pepper.

Indian Rice Pilau

Cooking time: 9 minutes
Serves 4 as a side dish

The brown basmati gives extra flavor and fiber, but takes a little longer to cook than regular rice. For extra color and crunch, finish this dish by adding your choice of raisins, currants, chopped red bell pepper or green onions.

Ingredients

1/4 cup (50 ml) butter
1 small onion, minced
4 green cardamom pods
1 cinnamon stick
1 bay leaf
1/2 teaspoon (2 ml) ground turmeric
1/2 teaspoon (2 ml) ground cumin
1-1/2 cups (375 ml) brown basmati rice
1/2 teaspoon (2 ml) salt
2 cups (500 ml) water or vegetable stock
1/2 cup (125 ml) raisins or currants and/or finely chopped red bell pepper and green onions to finish (optional)

Directions

In a pressure cooker, heat the butter over medium heat then add the onion, cardamom, cinnamon, bay leaf, turmeric and cumin and sauté until the onion is soft and the spices are fragrant.

Add the rice, stirring to coat then add the salt and water and bring to a boil.

Lock the lid in place and bring the cooker up to full pressure over high heat then reduce the heat to medium-low, just to maintain even pressure, and cook for 9 minutes.

Remove from heat and allow the pressure to drop naturally for 7 to 10 minutes then release any remaining pressure quickly.

Fluff the rice with a fork and discard the cinnamon stick and bay leaf.

If desired, stir in the raisins, currents, red pepper or green onions.

Wild Rice Casserole with Mixed Mushrooms and Chestnuts

Cooking time: 20 minutes
Serves 4

This side dish makes a great addition to Thanksgiving or Christmas dinner. For an interesting flavor variation, try replacing the mushrooms with dried fruits such as currants, apricots or cranberries.

Ingredients

2 tablespoons (25 ml) butter
1 onion, finely chopped
2 cloves garlic, minced
1 cup (250 ml) sliced mixed mushrooms (such as Portobello, oyster, shitake and white)
1 cup (250 ml) wild rice
1 cup (250 ml) cooked and crumbled chestnuts or 1/2 cup (125 ml) toasted pecans
2 sprigs thyme (or 1 teaspoon [5 ml] dried)
2 cups (500 ml) vegetable stock
Salt and freshly ground black pepper to taste

Directions

In a pressure cooker, melt the butter over medium heat then add the onion, garlic, and mushrooms and sauté until they start to brown.

Stir in the wild rice, chestnuts, thyme, and stock then bring to a boil.

Lock the lid in place and bring the cooker to full pressure over high heat then reduce the heat to medium-low, just to maintain even pressure, and cook for 20 minutes.

Remove from heat and allow the pressure to drop naturally.

The rice should be tender, with many of the grains broken and curled. If not, return to full pressure and cook for 2 to 3 minutes longer. Remove from heat and allow the pressure to drop naturally.

Drain off any excess liquid.

Discard the thyme sprigs and season to taste with salt and pepper.

Desserts

THE RECIPES

Poached Winter Fruit Compote

Cooking time: 1 minute
Serves 4 to 6

Serve this light and healthy fruit dessert with a dollop of lemon yogurt or crème fraiche*. It also makes a nice treat for brunch or spooned over pound cake.

Ingredients

3 firm cooking apples (such as Northern Spy or Rome Beauty)
3 firm, under-ripe pears (Bosc variety holds its shape best; or use Barrlett)
1 seedless orange
1 cup (250 ml) apple juice
1 cup (250 ml) dry white wine
2 tablespoons (25 ml) buckwheat honey (or other dark honey)
1 cinnamon stick
1/4 teaspoon (1 ml) ground nutmeg
Zest of 1 lemon, minced
1/2 cup (125 ml) dried cranberries or dried cherries
1/2 cup (125 ml) vanilla or lemon yogurt
Cinnamon for dusting

Directions

Peel and core the apples and pears and cut into wedges then set aside.

Remove the zest from the orange and set aside.

Cut peels from the orange and cut out segments then cover and refrigerate until serving.

In a pressure cooker, combine the apple juice, wine, honey, cinnamon stick and nutmeg and bring to a boil then reduce the heat and simmer for 1 minute.

Add the apple, pears, orange zest and lemon zest.

Lock the lid in place and bring the cooker up to full pressure over high heat then reduce the heat to medium-low, just to maintain even pressure, and cook for 1 minute.

Remove from heat and release the pressure quickly.

Using a slotted spoon, transfer the fruit to a bowl.

Bring the remaining syrup to a boil, and continue boiling to reduce and thicken.

Pour the syrup over the fruit and stir in the dried cranberries then cover and refrigerate overnight.

Stir in the orange segments.

Serve in individual bowls, each with a dollop of yogurt or crème fraiche* and a dusting of cinnamon.

* **_Note:_** Crème fraiche is made by combining 2 cups (500 ml) whipping (35%) cream with 1/2 cup (125 ml) sour cream, and letting the mixture stand at room temperature for 12 to 24 hours to thicken. Refrigerate the crème fraiche up to 2 weeks.

Creamy Rice Pudding with Sun-Dried Cranberries

Cooking time: 6 to 7 minutes
Serves 4 to 6

The pressure cooker is ideal for making risotto. And here we have a sweet version of the rice dish which, combined with milk and dried fruit, makes a deliciously comforting dessert.

Ingredients

1 cup (250 ml) Arborio or other short-grain rice
2 tablespoons (25 ml) butter
2 cups (500 ml) water
1 can (14 ounces [385 or 398 ml]) 2% evaporated milk
1/2 teaspoon (2 ml) ground cinnamon
1/4 teaspoon (1 ml) freshly grated nutmeg
1/2 cup (125 ml) dried cranberries, dried cherries or raisins
1/2 cup (125 ml) low-fat sweetened condensed milk
1 teaspoon (5 ml) vanilla extract

Directions

In a pressure cooker, melt the butter over medium heat then stir in the rice, coating the grains with the butter.

Stir in the water, evaporated milk, cinnamon and nutmeg and bring the mixture to a boil over medium heat, stirring to make sure the milk does not burn.

Lock the lid in place and bring the cooker up to full pressure over medium-high heat then reduce the heat to medium-low, just to maintain even pressure, and cook for 6 to 7 minutes.

Remove the cooker from the heat and allow the pressure to drop naturally for about 7 minutes then remove the lid.

Stir in the dried cranberries, condensed milk and vanilla then let stand, covered (do not lock), for 5 minutes.

Spoon the pudding into individual dishes and serve warm, or cover with plastic and chill to serve cold.

Poached Pears in Spiced Red Wine

Cooking time: 4 minutes
Serves 6

You can serve this easy-but-elegant fall dessert warm from the pan or chilled with a dollop of lemon yogurt. Be sure to use slightly, under-ripe pears and leave them whole, with stems intact, for a dramatic presentation.

Ingredients

6 firm, slightly under-ripe pears (preferably Bosc or Comice)
1 lemon
1/2 cup (125 ml) granulated sugar
3 whole cloves
1 cinnamon stick
2 cups (500 ml) light red wine
Lemon yogurt as accompaniment
Mint leaves for garnish

Directions

Peel the pears and, using an apple corer or small melon baller, remove the cores from the bottoms, leaving the stems intact and the pears whole. Cut a thin slice from the bottom of each pear so they will stand upright.

Using a vegetable peeler, remove the zest from the lemon in large strips and reserve the lemon for another use.

In a pressure cooker, combine the lemon zest, sugar, cloves, cinnamon and wine and cook over medium heat until the sugar is dissolved.

Stand the pears in the pot.

Lock the lid in place and bring the cooker up to full pressure over high heat then reduce the heat to medium-low just to maintain even pressure, and cook for 4 minutes.

Remove from heat and release the pressure quickly.

Remove the lid and let the pears cool in their liquid.

With a slotted spoon, carefully transfer the pears to a shallow dish.

Boil the poaching liquid over high heat until reduced, glossy and syrupy.

Spoon the syrup over the pears and cool slightly, or chill them overnight.

Serve the pears whole (or sliced lengthwise up to the stem and fanned) on individual dessert plates with some of the syrup drizzled over them.

If served cold, garnish with a dollop of lemon yogurt and mint leaf.

Lemon Cheesecake

Cooking time: 8 minutes
Serves 8

Serve this rich, popular dessert topped with cherry pie filling or sugared fresh blueberries, raspberries, or strawberries.

Ingredients

12 gingersnaps or vanilla wafers
1-1/2 tablespoons (22 ml) almonds, toasted
1/2 tablespoon (7 ml) butter, melted
2 8-ounce (250 g) packages cream cheese, room temperature
1/2 cup (125 ml) sugar
2 ounces (50 g) silken tofu
Zest of 1 lemon, grated
1 tablespoon (15 ml) fresh lemon juice
1/2 teaspoon (2ml) natural lemon extract
1 teaspoon (5 ml) vanilla
2 cups (500 ml) water

Directions

For this recipe, you need to use a pressure cooker with a rack that is large enough to hold a 7" × 3" (18 cm X 7.5 cm) spring-form pan. Treat the inside of the pan with nonstick spray.

Add the gingersnaps and almonds to a food processor and pulse to create crumbs then add the melted butter and pulse to mix.

Transfer the crumb mixture to the spring-form pan and press down into the pan.

Cut the cream cheese into cubes and add it to the food processor along with the sugar and process until smooth then add the silken tofu, lemon zest, lemon juice, lemon extract, and vanilla and process the mixture for 10 seconds.

Scrape the bowl and then process for another 10 seconds or until the batter is well mixed and smooth.

Place the spring-form pan in the center of two 16" × 16" (40 cm X 40 cm) pieces of aluminum foil then crimp the foil to seal the bottom of the pan.

Transfer the cheesecake batter into the spring-form pan.

Treat one side of a 10" (25 cm) square of aluminum foil with nonstick spray and lay over the top of the spring-form pan and crimp around the edges.

Bring the bottom foil up the sides so that it can be grasped to raise and lower the pan in and out of the pressure cooker.

Pour the water into the pressure cooker then insert the rack and set the spring-form pan holding the cheesecake batter on the rack.

Lock the lid into place, bring to high pressure and maintain the pressure for 8 minutes.

Remove from heat and allow pressure to release naturally.

Remove the lid and lift the covered spring-form pan out of the pressure cooker and place on a wire rack then remove the top foil.

If any moisture has accumulated on top of the cheesecake, dab it with a piece of paper towel to remove it.

Let cool to room temperature and then remove from the spring-form pan.

Stocks, Sauces and Condiments

THE RECIPES

Vegetable Stock

Cooking time: 15 minutes
Makes 6 to 8 cups (1.5 to 2 L)

You can use clean peelings from carrots and parsnips in this vegetarian stock.

Ingredients

2 tablespoons (25 ml) butter or olive oil
4 cloves garlic, peeled
3 sprigs parsley
2 carrots, scrubbed and chopped
2 stalks celery, coarsely chopped
1 large onion, quartered
1 parsnips, scrubbed and chopped
1 tomato, chopped
1 bay leaf
1 sprig thyme
8 cups (2 L) water

Directions

In a pressure cooker, heat the butter over medium heat then add the garlic, parsley, carrots, celery, onion, parsnips, tomato, bay leaf and thyme and sauté for 10 minutes or until softened.

Pour in the water.

Lock the lid in place and bring the cooker up to full pressure over high heat then reduce the heat to medium-low, just to maintain even pressure, and cook for 15 minutes.

Remove from heat and allow the pressure to drop naturally.

Strain the stock through a fine mesh sieve or cheese cloth, pressing on the solids to release all of their liquid then discard the solids.

Basic Tomato and Vegetable Sauce for Pasta

Cooking time: 8 minutes
Makes 4 to 5 cups (1 to 1.25 L)

This versatile pasta sauce will keep for 3 days in the refrigerator or up to 3 months in the freezer.

Ingredients

1/4 cup (50 ml) olive oil
1 cup (250 ml) chopped onions
3 cloves garlic, minced
1 small zucchini, chopped
1 large carrot, chopped
1 cup (250 ml) chopped eggplant
1/2 cup (125 ml) chopped red or yellow bell peppers
1/2 cup (125 ml) chopped fresh mushrooms
1 can (25 ounces [796 ml]) crushed tomatoes
1 teaspoon (5 ml) dried oregano
1 teaspoon (5 ml) dried basil
1/4 cup (50 ml) tomato paste
1 teaspoon (5 ml) granulated sugar
1/4 teaspoon (1 ml) red pepper flakes
Salt and freshly ground black pepper to taste

Directions

In a pressure cooker, heat the oil over medium-high heat then add the onion and garlic and sauté until they start to brown.

Stir in the zucchini, carrot, eggplant, peppers, and mushrooms and cook for 5 minutes longer.

Add the tomatoes, oregano and basil.

Lock the lid in place and bring the cooker up to full pressure over high heat then reduce the heat to medium-low, just to maintain even pressure, and cook for 8 minutes.

~ 103 ~

Remove from heat and allow the pressure to drop naturally.

Stir in the tomato paste. (If desired, purée some or all of the sauce with an immersion blender or in a food processor.)

Stir in the sugar and red pepper flakes then season to taste with salt and pepper.

Cowboy Ranchero Sauce

Cooking time: 7 minutes
Makes 4 to 5 cups (1 to 1.25 L)

Use this southwestern vegetarian sauce over pasta or spooned over enchiladas before baking.

Ingredients

16 plum tomatoes (about 4 pounds [2 kg]), cored and halved
12 serrano chilies, seeded and halved
6 cloves garlic, peeled
2 large sweet onions, chopped
1 cup (250 ml) beer
2 tablespoons (25 ml) honey (or to taste)
Salt to taste
1 cup (250 ml) chopped cilantro leaves

Directions

In a pressure cooker, combine the tomato, chilies, garlic, onions and beer.

Lock the lid in place and bring the cooker up to full pressure over high heat then reduce the heat to medium-low, just to maintain even pressure, and cook for 7 minutes.

Remove from heat and release the pressure quickly.

Strain the sauce through a sieve, reserving the liquid.

Transfer the solids to a food processor and purée until smooth then return to the cooker and add honey to taste.

Stir in enough of the reserved liquid to create a smooth sauce then season to taste with salt.

Stir in the cilantro just before serving.

Strawberry Jam

Cooking time: 7 minutes
Makes 4 cups (1 L)

The pressure cooker makes this smooth textured jam so quickly; all of the intense strawberry color is preserved. If you have a 6-litre machine, you can easily double this recipe.

Ingredients

4 cups (1 L) hulled strawberries, halved
3 cups (750 ml) granulated sugar
Juice of 1 lemon

Directions

In a pressure cooker, combine the strawberries and sugar then let stand for 30 to 60 minutes, until juicy.

Using a potato masher, mash the fruit, making sure all of the sugar is dissolved then stir in the lemon juice and bring to a boil.

Lock the lid in place and bring the cooker up to full pressure over high heat then reduce the heat to medium-low, just to maintain even pressure, and cook for 7 minutes.

Remove the cooker from the heat and allow the pressure to drop naturally.

Remove the lid then bring to a rapid boil over high heat and boil, uncovered, for about 3 minutes, or just until the jam reaches the gel stage (when a bit spooned onto an ice-cold plate sets up and congeals).

Skim off any foam and ladle into hot sterilized jars, leaving 1/2 inch (1 cm) head space then seal the jars.

Cool and refrigerate up to 1 week, freeze for up to 1 month, or process for shelf storage.

Fresh Apricot Jam

Cooking time: 8 minutes
Makes 6 to 7 cups (1.5 to 1.75 L)

This recipe makes a very smooth, softly-set apricot jam, perfect for glazing fruit tarts or other desserts. If you prefer a chunkier jam, only purée a portion of the fresh apricots with the orange flesh in the food processor.

Ingredients

6 cups (1.5 L) apricots, halved
1 large navel orange, peeled
1/2 cup (125 ml) water or apple juice
6 cups (1.5 L) granulated sugar

Directions

In a food processor, chop the apricots and orange with water, in batches if necessary, then pour into a pressure cooker.

Stir in the sugar and let stand for 30 minutes then bring to a boil, stirring until the sugar is dissolved.

Lock the lid in place and bring the cooker up to full pressure over high heat then reduce the heat to medium-low, just to maintain even pressure, and cook for 8 minutes.

Remove from heat and allow the pressure to drop naturally.

Remove the lid then bring to a rapid boil over high heat and boil, uncovered, for about 3 minutes, or just until the jam reaches the gel stage (when a bit spooned onto ice-cold plate sets up and congeals).

Skim off any foam and ladle into hot sterilized jars, leaving 1/2 inch (1 cm) head space then seal the jars.

Cool and refrigerate up to 1 week, freeze for up to 1 month, or process for shelf storage.

Spiced Dried Apricot Jam

Cooking time: 10 minutes
Makes about 7 cups (1.75 L)

The aromatic spices in this jam give it a lovely flavor and aroma. It's delicious on scones for breakfast.

Ingredients

4 cups (1 L) dried apricots, coarsely chopped
2 cups (500 ml) water
6 black peppercorns
5 cardamom pods
2 cinnamon sticks
2 star anise or 1 teaspoon (5 ml) anise or fennel seed
Juice of 2 lemons
4 cups (1 L) granulated sugar

Directions

In a bowl, combine the apricots and water then cover and let soak for 24 hours.

In a square of cheesecloth, wrap the peppercorns, cardamom pods, cinnamon sticks and star of anise
and tie into a bag with kitchen string. (Or place the ingredients in a tea ball).

Add the apricots and spice bag to the pressure cooker then stir in the lemon juice.

Lock the lid in place and bring the cooker up to full pressure over high heat then reduce the heat to medium-low, just to maintain even pressure, and cook for 10 minutes.

Remove from heat and allow the pressure to drop naturally.

Discard the spice bag then stir in the sugar and bring to a rapid boil over high heat and boil, uncovered for about 3 to 4 minutes, until the gel point is reached (when a bit spooned onto an ice-cold plate sets up and congeals).

Skim off any foam and ladle into hot sterilized jars, leaving 1/2 inch (1 cm) head space then seal the jars.

Cool and refrigerate up to 1 week, freeze for up to 1 month, or process for shelf storage.

Mixed Berry and Red Fruit Jam

Cooking time: 10 minutes
Makes 6 cups (1.5 L)

Use fresh or frozen fruit for this rich, inky, mixed-berry jam. If you like, substitute chopped prunes or dark raisins for the black currants.

Ingredients

1 pounds (500 g) cranberries
8 ounces (250 g) raspberries
8 ounces (250 g) blueberries
8 ounces (250 g) strawberries, chopped
4 ounces (125 g) rhubarb, chopped
4 ounces (125 g) dried black currant
Zest and juice of 1 lemon
6 cups (1.5 L) granulated sugar

Directions

In a pressure cooker, combine the cranberries, raspberries, blueberries, strawberries, rhubarb, black currants, lemon zest, lemon juice, and sugar and let stand for 30 to 60 minutes until juicy.

Bring to a boil, adding up to 1/4 cup (50 ml) water if necessary to dissolve the sugar.

Lock the lid in place and bring the cooker up to full pressure over high heat then reduce the heat to medium-low, just to maintain even pressure, and cook for 10 minutes.

Remove from heat and allow the pressure to drop naturally.

Remove the lid then boil the jam rapidly for about 3 to 4 minutes, until the gel point is reached (when a bit spooned onto an ice-cold plate sets up and congeals).

Skim off any foam and ladle into hot sterilized jars leaving 1/2 inch (1 cm) head space then seal the jars.

Cool and refrigerate up to 1 week, freeze for up to 1 month, or process for shelf storage.

Pear Mincemeat

Cooking time: 10 minutes
Makes 5 cups (1.25 L)

Use a heavy, covered canner or stock pot for processing preserves. If you don't have a proper canner (with a wire lifting insert) place a metal rack in the bottom of the pot. The canner or pot should be large enough so that when submerged, jars will be covered by about 1 inch (2 cm) of boiling water.

Ingredients

2-1/2 pounds (1.25 kg) pears, peeled, cored and chopped
1 green apple, peeled, cored and chopped
Zest and juice of 1 lemon
Zest and juice of 1 orange
1 cup (250 ml) golden raisins
1/2 cup (125 ml) dried cranberries or currants
1/2 cup (125 ml) packed brown sugar
1 teaspoon (5 ml) ground cinnamon
1 teaspoon (5 ml) ground nutmeg
1/4 teaspoon (1 ml) ground ginger
Pinch of salt
1/2 cup (125 ml) chopped walnuts or pecans, toasted
1/2 cup (125 ml) cognac or pear brandy

Directions

In a pressure cooker, combine the pears, apple, lemon zest, lemon juice, orange zest, orange juice, raisins, cranberries, sugar, cinnamon, nutmeg, ginger, and salt then bring to a boil over medium heat.

Lock the lid in place and bring the cooker up to full pressure over high heat then reduce the heat to medium-low, just to maintain even pressure, and cook for 10 minutes.

Remove from heat and allow the pressure to drop naturally.

Simmer, uncovered, for 10 minutes or until the mixture is very thick then stir in the walnuts and cognac and cook for 5 minutes longer.

Ladle into hot, sterilized jars, leaving 1/2 inch (1 cm) head space then seal the jars.

Cool and refrigerate, freeze, or process in a boiling water bath for shelf storage.

Conclusion

I sincerely hope that these recipes will help you discover and appreciate the amazing versatility of the pressure cooker! And remember, your imagination is the only limit when it comes to creating delicious pressure cooked vegetarian meals. Don't be afraid to adapt your recipes to taste and to try different combination of spices.

If you enjoyed this cookbook, then you may also enjoy my other books:

- Vegetarian Slow Cooker Recipe Book: 30 Easy Set It & Forget It Meals
- Pressure Cooker Recipe Book: Fast Cooking Under Extreme Pressure
- Slow Cooker International Cooking: A Culinary Journey of Set It & Forget It Meals
- 5 Ingredients 15 Minutes Prep Time Slow Cooker Cookbook: Quick & Easy Set It & Forget It Recipes
- Vegetarian Slow Cooker Recipes: Top 71 Quick & Easy Vegetarian Crockpot Recipe Book
- 4 Ingredients or Less Cookbook: Fast, Practical & Healthy Meal Options
- Gluten-Free Diet Cookbook: Healthier Eating Choices for People with Celiac Disease
- Satisfying Slow Cooker Meals and More

For more information about myself and to enjoy more amazing recipes, please follow these links:

- Maria Holmes author page at www.Amazon.com
- www.holmescookedmeals.com
- Holmes Cooked Meals Facebook page

I will be writing and publishing more cookbooks in the future, so please stay tuned. But for now, I would like to thank you for helping me and supporting my efforts to share my passion for cooking.

Index

Printed in Great Britain
by Amazon